PHILIP SCHNEIDER

The life and death of one of the bravest whistleblowers of the 20th century

Copyright 2018 by Arthur Berkeley

Revised edition 2020

All rights reserved

No part of this publication may be reproduced

INTRODUCTION

1 The early years – Oscar Schneider
2 The Philadelphia Experiment
3 US government geologist and engineer, DUMBS
4 Dulce Alien War, August 1979, NM
5 Lecture Tours
6 Phil Schneider's assassination, January 1996
7 Al Bielek's assessment of Phil Schneider
8 Hale-Bopp Comet and Al Bielek
9 The Montauk Project
10 New World Order Agenda
11 Epilogue

INTRODUCTION

Philip Schneider was a controversial figure, who exposed the US government's involvement with UFOs and extraterrestrials. As a government geologist and engineer, he was involved in the construction of Deep Underground Military Bases, known as DUMBS. He also held an important position in NATO, and eventually resigned forfeiting a $1,000,000 pension per annum.

For two years before his death, Phil Schneider gave a series of lectures, touring the United States. He spoke about the government cover-ups, black budgets, and secret extraterrestrial agreements that circumvented the American constitution. An enigmatic figure, Phil Schneider was not frightened to tell the world the truth. His video's bear witness to the appalling injuries he sustained, during the Dulce-Alien war of August 1979. In the battle 66 workers and military personnel were killed, Phil Schneider being one of only three survivors.

During the lectures Phil Schneider was able to provide incontrovertible proof, that the US government was involved in an appalling cover-up of UFOs and black projects. He displayed special metals, which were of alien origin, and photographs of the DUMBS.

Phil Schneider had a level 3 security clearance, Rhydite 38, that allowed him to work at Area 51, S4, and Los Alamos. As a government geologist and engineer, Phil worked for 17 years on black projects. After attending two sessions of top secret UN meetings at an underground base outside New York, he resigned his position in complete disgust of the 'alien agenda' of the New World Order.

Phil Schneider was assassinated in January 1996. The official version was that he committed suicide, but this was proven to be impossible, due to his physical disabilities. Prior to his death there had been numerous attempts on his life by intelligence agencies. Most people including his ex-wife Cynthia Drayer, now believe that Phil Schneider was murdered for publicly revealing the truth about the US government's cover-up of black projects and secret extraterrestrial agreements.

THE EARLY YEARS – OSCAR SCHNEIDER

Philip Schneider was born on April 23, 1947, at Bethesda Navy Hospital. Oscar and Sally Schneider were Philip's parents. Oscar Schneider was born in Germany, and was the captain of a U boat in the German navy during World War two. He was responsible for sinking allied ships during the early part of the war. It is estimated that he had sunk 68 British and French ships, by the time he was captured by the French in 1940. He was eventually handed over to the Americans, and given the same rank as captain in the American navy. This bizarre situation has never been fully explained, but it was known that Oscar Schneider had been working on time travel experiments in a top secret German program.

Allegedly the Germans had been successful with time travel experiments before the second world war was over. The assumption is that the US government needed Oscar Schneider's knowledge, and he was assigned immediately to the Philadelphia Experiment in late 1941. Oscar was appointed chief medical officer for the experiment.

He also helped to design the first nuclear submarines, and took part in Operation Crossroads, which was the testing of nuclear weapons at Bikini Island, in the south pacific.

Phil knew that his father Oscar Schneider had been involved in the Philadelphia Experiment, before he died of cancer, but he didn't know his father's true history. It was only when Oscar knew he was dying, that he told Phil the truth. Two weeks prior to Oscar's death, Phil learnt that his father was born in Germany in 1905, and not in the US, California. Phil Schneider was surprised that his father suddenly became a medical doctor. The US Navy made up the whole story, so that Oscar could become involved with the Philadelphia Experiment immediately. His advanced knowledge of mathematical equations for time travel, and his involvement in the German programme, were the main reasons why the US government wanted him.

THE PHILADELPHIA EXPERIMENT

The Philadelphia Experiment is purported to have taken place at the Philadelphia Naval Shipyard in Pennsylvania on October 28, 1943. Invisibility experiments were conducted aboard USS Eldridge, resulting in the full scale teleportation of the destroyer and its crew through both time and space. The Philadelphia experiment was initially conceived as an invisibility to radar project, and it was known as 'Project Rainbow'.

It is believed that the experiment was based on unified field theory, a term used by Albert Einstein. This describes both mathematically and physically, the nature of the forces of electromagnetic radiation and gravity, and unites the fields of electromagnetism and gravity into a single field. Some researchers have hypothesized that some version of the field would enable, using large electrical generators, which would bend light around an object via refraction, rendering the object completely invisible. Naturally the Navy would regard this of military value, and in all probability sponsored the experiment.

The first experiment began in June 1943, and the USS Eldridge was equipped with an array of electronic equipment. The test resulted in the USS Eldridge being rendered nearly invisible, and being engulfed in a mysterious green mist. When the ship reappeared, some of the sailors were reported embedded in the metal structure of the ship. And one sailor ended up on a deck below where he began, and his hand was embedded in the steel hull of the ship. Other sailors suffered severe nausea, and some went completely mad. At this stage the experiment was altered by the Navy, with the new objective to render the USS Eldridge solely invisible to radar.

The experiment was repeated on October 28, 1943. With this experiment he USS Eldridge became invisible, disappearing from radar, in a flash of blue light. It teleported to Norfolk, Virginia, 320 km, where it stayed for several minutes, before returning to Philadelphia in another flash. It was seen by members of the crew on the ship SS Furuseth, in Virginia. On returning to Philadelphia, the USS Eldridge had gone back approximately 10 minutes in time. Some crew members had mental disorders, others were fused to the ship's metal, an some were even missing altogether.

Al Bielek, a close friend of Phil Schneider, claimed that he was a crew member of the USS Eldridge, and took part in the experiment. Bielek's version of events differs slightly, in that he claims the USS Eldridge was teleported to Montauk, Long Island. It was purported to have travelled through a time-portal, and arrived in 1983. Dr Von Neuman, the director of 'Project Rainbow', greeted some of the crew, before sending them back to 1943.

In 1979 the linguist Charles Berlitz, with co-author William L.Moore, published 'The Philadelphia Experiment: Project Invisibility'. And in 1984, a time travel film called The Philadelphia Experiment, directed by Stewart Raffill, was released.

US GOVERNMENT GEOLOGIST AND ENGINEER

Philip Schneider was a US government geologist and engineer, who was involved in the construction of deep underground military bases, known as DUMBS. Schneider was a black operations whistleblower, who exposed the truth about the cover-up of these DUMBS, and the secret agreements with extraterrestrials. For 17 years Schneider worked as a geologist, and structural engineer building DUMBS in America, and many countries worldwide. These underground military bases cost between 17 and 19 billion dollars each, at the time of his death in January 1996. Phil purported that there were 131 in the US, and 1,477 worldwide. He said that most bases were over 2 miles deep, and that Magnetic-Levatation trains connected all DUMBS. These trains can reach a speed of Mach 2 or more. Schneider helped to construct this subterranean transport system.

The deep underground bases were constructed by using nuclear powered machines, TBMs, which are able to melt rock, leaving behind glass like walls. They can tunnel up to two miles a day. Phil Schneider, being one of the leading US geologists, was required to ascertain the explosives needed for the particular kind of rocks. DUMBS were usually constructed under military bases. However, the deep underground military base below Denver Airport, consisted of eight levels.

Apart from being a US government geologist and structural engineer, Phil Schneider held a high level position in NATO. This enabled him to travel to many different countries. In Russia he discovered that there had been many UFO crashes, similar to the US. Many of these spacecraft had been shot down by the military.

The most significant UFO crash in America was the Roswell UFO crash of July 1947. Three alien bodies were found, and one live alien. These were short Greys, the spacecraft was taken first to Wright Patterson AFB, Dayton, Ohio, then to Area 51, Nevada. The saucer was eventually reversed engineered. In 1954 President Eisenhower signed the Greada Treaty with the Greys. In exchange for military technology, the US allowed the Greys to abduct humans for genetic experiments and implants. Initially the Greys were required to supply the US government with a list of those humans abducted, which were several thousand per year. However, it soon became clear that the Greys had violated the treaty, abducting more people than they claimed, and had not returned them to their place of abduction. A part of the treaty was to provide the Greys with deep underground bases.

Phil Schneider was invited to attend a top secret UN meeting at one of these underground military bases, outside New York. He attended two sessions, and discovered that 5 Tall Grey extraterrestrials were dictating policies to the UN. It was this incident that led Phil Schneider to relinquish his position as a US government geologist. The whole geology department of 40 members also walked out. He felt that the alien ' New World Order agenda', had got so far out of hand, that the American constitution no longer had any legal standing. International leaders were literally at the mercy of the Greys.

DULCE ALIEN WAR, NEW MEXICO, AUGUST 1979

In August 1979, Philip Schneider was involved in building an extension to the deep underground base at Dulce, New Mexico. At the time he was employed by Morrison-Knudsen, Inc. The base goes down seven levels, and is over 2.5 miles deep. The project at the time had drilled four holes in the desert, which had to be linked together with tunnels. Schneider's job was to descend the holes, to check the rock samples, and determine the explosives that were needed to deal with the particular kind of rock. As Schneider and his team went down, they discovered a large cavern full of aliens, known as Tall Greys. Schneider shot two Greys, and 40 more people came down, who were all killed in the firefight. They had opened a large cavern, which was a secret base for the Greys. Altogether 66 workers and military personnel were killed. Phil

Schneider suffered appalling injuries, he was shot in the chest with one of their beam weapons. His fingers were burnt off, as well as toes from one foot.

Phil also had a dose of cobalt radiation, which eventually caused him to develop cancer. He was only one of three people to survive the incident. His appalling injuries can be clearly seen in his videos, and he frequently showed the scar on his chest at lectures. The other two survivors were Canadians, and lived in a retirement home in Canada, and were not allowed any visitors.

Phil Schneider claimed to have worked on 13 US DUMBS. Two of these bases were major ones, Area 51 and Dulce, New Mexico. Schneider asserted that Gray humanoid extraterrestrials worked alongside American personnel. The Dulce base being a biogenetic laboratory, where human-alien, and human-animal hybrids were created.

It took Phil Schneider two years to recuperate after the 1979 Dulce incident. He went back to work for Morrison and Knudson, EG & G and other companies.

The Dulce base is one of the deepest underground military bases in the US. It consists of seven levels, at a depth of over two and a half miles. The levels of Dulce Airbase comprise:

Level 1   Security & Communications

Level 2   Human Staff housing

Level 3   Laboratories

Level 4   Mind Control Experiments

Level 5   Alien Housing

Level 6   Genetic Experiments

Level 7   Cryogenic Storage

There have been several other whistleblowers, most notably Thomas Edwin Castello. He claimed to be a former security officer, who was employed by the Rand Corporation, at the Dulce underground base. Castello has not come forward in person, and it may be that this is a fictitious name used by a whistleblower who worked at the base. Castello claimed that the Tall Greys, and the Dracos worked at Dulce, together with 18,000 short Greys living at the facility. The Greys and Draconians are highly developed technologically, but have no ethical or moral standards in performing atrocious genetic experiments on humans and animals.

Thomas Castello had a ULTRA-7 clearance, which allowed him access to all 7 levels. The majority of aliens were on levels 5,6 and 7. The main alien housing being on level 5. Level 6 is known as 'Nightmare Hall'. It holds genetic laboratories, where experiments are done on a variety of animals and humans, creating hybrid races. There are human-animal hybrids, and human-alien hybrids. On level 7, Castello encountered humans in cages, rows of thousands of humans, men, women and children. Embryos of humanoids being kept in cold storage. The humans in cages were frequently drugged, many were crying out for help. Castello was told that they were insane, and drug tests were carried out on them to cure their insanity. Castello was told never to speak to them.

Castello is alleged to have stolen the 'Dulce Papers', a video tape and 30 black and white photos. It is believed that Castello moved to Costa Rica. Castello asserted that his wife and son are missing, and maybe in an underground base. Castello also went missing, and it is not known if he is still alive.

LECTURE TOURS

For the last two years of his life, Phil Schneider had been on lecture tours. In his lectures he gave incontrovertible proof of US government cover-ups, black budgets, UFOs and secret alien agreements.

It was Phil Schneider's friend Al Bielek who suggested to Phil that he should go on a lecture circuit. His first attempt was on 7th May 1995 in Las Vegas, Nevada. Altogether Phil done over 30 lectures. However, the first one that was recorded was on 8th May 1995, at Post Falls, Idaho. Subsequent lecture tours included Denver, Colorado in August, Seattle in September, and Denver in November. In fact this was the last one that was recorded.

Many topics were dealt with in his lectures. In the 8th May lecture at Post Falls, Idaho, Phil spoke about railroad cars. He knew someone who lived near him in Portland, Ohio. Phil's friend worked at Gunderson Steel Fabrication, where they constructed railroad cars. He had known Phil for nearly 30 years, and he told Phil that they were 'prisoner cars'. The US government had a contract with Gunderson, to build 107,200 railroad cars, each fitted with 143 pairs of shackles. There were eleven sub-contractors involved in the programme. Gunderson received more than 2 billion dollars for the contract. Bethlehem Steel were also involved. Phil's friend showed him one of the cars in the rail yards in North Portland. Phil believed that up to 15 million people could be taken prisoner, and incarcerated indefinitely.

Another important topic dealt with in the lecture was 'Star Wars and the alien threat'. Phil asserted that 68% of the military budget is affected by the black budget. The SDI or 'Star Wars' relies mainly upon stealth weaponry. The whole programme derived from the reverse-engineering of crashed alien discs.

Phil believed that the 'Star Wars' programme was used as a buffer to prevent an alien attack. The whole programme had nothing to do with the cold war with Russia. In fact Gorbachev knew about the alien cover-up, when he met Reagan at the Reykjavik summit in 1986.

Other topics discussed were various alien metals, some of which were exhibited at his lectures. Phil also asserted that he had crashed retrievable metals from the Roswell UFO crash in New Mexico, which were given to him when he was 14 years old.

He also displayed a special titanium alloy, which was originally used in the SR 71 Blackbird, and F1 17A stealth fighter. He described these as older technologies, and they were working on a new class of hypersonic aircraft, above Mach 5. He also stated that they employ modern charged particle beam weapons, rather than lasers.

Phil also disclosed a new kind of infrared technology for a satellite 150,000 miles out in a geosynchronous orbit. It has incredible surveillance capabilities, and can literally see a dime on the kitchen floor!

He displayed various other metals, some of which were obtained from Tall Grey technologies, and could withstand temperatures of 10,000 degrees Fahrenheit. These materials Phil had worked on daily, as he was involved in the construction of the first stealth fighter and bomber, he participated in the secret military programme.

PHIL SCHNEIDER'S ASSASSINATION, JANUARY 1996

Phil Schneider was assassinated in January, 1996. There had been several attempts on his life by the FBI, and he was finally assassinated on or about the 12th January. The previous year in September 1995, Schneider was shot in the shoulder by an FBI agent. Schneider claimed that he shot the FBI agent in self defence. Prior to his death, Phil Schneider was renting an apartment in Willsonville, Oregon. Phil had been friendly with a religious group, and one of their members Al Pratt visited Phil regularly. For several days in succession Al went to Phil's apartment, but there was no reply when Al went to his door. Subsequently Al Pratt contacted the County Sheriff's office, a detective and the manager of the Autumn Park Apartments entered Phil's apartment. Inside they discovered Phil Schneider's body, he had been dead for approximately seven days. The County Coroner's office attributed Phil Schneider's death to a stroke. In the days following his death, new evidence began to surface, which led some people to believe that Phil Schneider did not die from a stroke, but he had actually been murdered.

Detective Randy Harris contacted Phil's ex-wife Cynthia Drayer, and told her that something was wrong, and that there were marks on Phil's neck. His body was subsequently removed from the funeral home, and an autopsy carried out by Dr Karen Gunson. The autopsy revealed that the cause of death was a rubber hose, which had been wrapped three times around his neck, and tied in a knot. The conclusion of the autopsy was that he had committed suicide.

When Philip's body was discovered, it was in an unusual position. The feet were under the bed, his head in the wheelchair seat, the rest of the body on the floor, with his hands by his sides. There was blood on the floor near the wheelchair, but no blood was found on the wheelchair. There were no wounds on Phil's body, to account for the blood. A sample of the blood was not taken, due to the belief that Phil had died of natural causes. And no suicide note was found. One of Phil's friends, Mark Rufener, said that he had seen Phil the weekend of January 6th and 7th, 1996. They were going to buy land in Colorado, and Phil had asked Mark to help him write a book about his knowledge of UFOs and aliens, One World government, and the Black Budget. As Mark said, ' Phil didn't commit suicide, he was murdered, and it was made to look like a suicide'.

Phil frequently ate out at the 76 Truck Stop in Aurora, Oregon. Donna, a waitress who worked at the restaurant, said Phil would often talk about his work, and that there had been many attempts to stop him talking. Donna asserted that Phil had a mission to talk about government cover-ups regarding UFOs and aliens, and that intelligence agencies intended to stop people who talked.

Phil Schneider's ex-wife Cynthia, believed that he was murdered. She thought that someone that Phil knew met him, and injected him with a drug to incapacitate him. The assailants then wrapped a rubber hose around his neck, tied it in a knot, asphyxiating him. Phil had three fingers missing on each hand, and it would be extremely difficult for him to do this. He could not manipulate his fingers. Phil Schneider would not commit suicide, he had everything to live for, especially his 8 year old daughter.

Several friends told Cynthia that they had seen Phil with a blonde woman, a few weeks before he died. During the course of a meeting with friends, Cynthia saw a blonde woman in a car with a pair of binoculars, watching the meeting through a window. When Cynthia approached the car, it quickly sped away. She was able to trace the license plate number, which turned out to be from a truck, where the plate number had been stolen. Cynthia's mother consulted a psychic medium, who told her that a woman who wore a blonde wig was involved in Phil's death. There had been 13 previous attempts on Phil's life by the FBI, before they finally succeeded in assassinating him.

AL BIELEK'S ASSESSMENT OF PHIL SCHNEIDER

Al Bielek and Phil Schneider were close personal friends. Al knew Phil Schneider several years prior to his death in 1996. In early 1993, Al Bielek was giving a lecture on the Philadelphia Experiment in Seattle, when Phil Schneider introduced himself and told Al Bielek that his father was Oscar Schneider, who was part of the Philadelphia Experiment. Al seemed to think that there might have been a connection between his father Alexander Duncan Cameron, and Oscar Schneider. Alexander Cameron had been involved in government intelligence, and was heavily involved in Operation Paperclip in 1946, and brought a lot of German scientists into the US. Al confirmed that he didn't know who they all were. Phil's father and Al's father were very close friends, even going on fishing trips together in Florida, after the end of the war.

Al Bielek's hypothesis is that his father knew Oscar Schneider, before he came to America. Phil initially approached Al, because he knew that Al was involved in the Philadelphia Experiment, together with his father Oscar. Phil and Al eventually became close friends. It was Al that persuaded Phil to get his knowledge of the Philadelphia Experiment, the underground bases, and the underground tube system, out to the public. Phil decided to go public in early 1995, and started the lecture circuit in May that year.

Phil also disclosed information about the Kobe earthquake in Japan, 1995. The death toll was over 4,000. He asserted that the earthquake was caused by a nuclear bomb, planted in the harbour by US Navy seals. Phil stated that there had been a long argument between the US and Japan regarding synthetic intelligence computer technology. Japan was a world leader with this technology. The attack was retribution by the US government, or at least by an element of the state.

Phil was invited to go to Japan by leading corporations, but the state department refused to let him go. Phil crossed over the border to Canada, and the Japanese flew a private plane to Vancouver to collect him. Phil spent three days in Japan lecturing about the Kobe earthquake. On his return to the US, Phil was visited by intelligence agents, who told him he had done major damage to the whole infrastructure, the New World Order. They invited him to come back and work for the government, but Phil refused. Shortly after this the FBI began assassination attempts on his life. Phil had stated that he wanted to put everything on record, because he had only told 1% of the story. At the time of his death Phil was working on a book, which would give the latitude and longitude of every Deep Underground Military Base. The manuscript was never found.

Although some people may have thought that Phil was a little odd, Al Bielek believed that Phil was a credible person, very sane and stable, and that he backed up all of his statements with some kind of evidence. By going public, Phil knew that his life was in jeopardy, which he had been told many times. Phil had an important mission, he had to get the truth out to the world.

HALE-BOPP COMET AND AL BIELEK

According to Al Bielek, the Hale-Bopp comet of 1997 could have collided with Earth. It was purported by Bielek that the comet was being followed by an object. Apparently NASA had known about this since 1997, and had kept it hidden from the public. In his book, 'The Day After Roswell', Col Philip Corso asserted that NASA was controlled by the CIA since 1961, so it wasn't independent.

NASAs predicted trajetion which it followed, meant that the comet would crash into the Earth. The 50 km wide

Hale-Bopp comet would have destroyed all life on Earth. Bielek stated that the US Air Force deflected the comet, and destroyed the object following it, by using particle beam weapons. Particle beam weapons in Scalar mode, are used to bring down UFOs. There is a special unit within NATO, Group 58, that retrieves crashed UFOs and alien bodies.

Several other astronomers have corroborated this, regarding an object following the Hale-Bopp comet. In November 1996, Chuck Shramek, and amateur astronomer of Houston, Texas, took a CCD image of the comet, which showed a slightly elongated object following it. Subsequently Shramet contacted Art Bell's radio program Coast to Coast AM, and announced that there was an object following the Hale-Bopp comet. Art Bell had also claimed to have obtained an image of the spacecraft from an anonymous astrophysicist.

Courtney Brown, a UFO enthusiast and professor at Emory University, concluded that there was an alien spacecraft following the comet.

THE MONTAUK PROJECT

The Montauk Project was the most amazing and secretive project ever undertaken by man. It started with the Philadelphia Experiment in 1943, an invisibility to radar project, and developed into a mind control and time travel project. The Montauk Project was run jointly by the USAF and Navy at Camp Hero, Montauk Point, Long Island, New York. This took place mainly during the 1970s and 1980s, although initial work began in 1968. Jack Pruitt, controlled the Montauk Project. Teenage boys were abducted for the terrible mind control experiments. Extraterrestrial races that were working with the US government, were involved with the time travel and mind control programme.

Preston Nichols, Duncan Cameron and Al Bielek were key participants in the Montauk Project. Al Bielek , an electronic engineer, together with his brother Duncan Cameron were recruited into the Montauk Project. Preston Nichols was also an electronic engineer. His involvement with Montauk began in 1968, and was informed that the research began immediately after the Philadelphia Experiment. Al Bielek was program director for the psychics who manned the Montauk Chair during the 1970s. He was in charge of the Mind Control program, and in contact with both Duncan Cameron and Preston Nichols. Stewart Swerdlow was one of the Montauk Boys, involved in mind control experiments under Al Bielek. Altogether about 30 people worked at Montauk.

The original funding came from a Nazi government fund, that is from gold bullion which was stolen near the end of WW2 in 1944. Operation Paperclip had brought German scientists over to the US in 1946. From 1968 to 1976 a German group funded the programme.

At the same time aliens worked with personnel on the base, to give technical assistance. During this period they were building hardware underground, and the alien contribution was of paramount importance. The objective of the time travel programme was to explore time and space to the fullest extent possible, and to travel from Point A to Point B through Hyperspace or a Wormhole. According to Al Bielek several extraterrestrial races are believed to have been involved with the project, including the Leverons, Reptilians, Tall Greys, Pleiadians, Aliens from Sirius, aliens from Sirius A, and Antarians. A Draconian was in overhall charge, who co-ordinated the alien effort. The Leverons from the Orion Confederation were computer experts, and they used their own computer systems, because the IBM computers at the time were not compatible with theirs.

It took nearly 10 years to get the first working time travel system, which was in 1977. A time tunnel was created, enabling a person to enter a wormhole in hyperspace. In the initial stages of the project, animals were put into the tunnels, then finally humans. There were many disasters, and some people never returned from the tunnel. From 1980 onwards the project was running smoothly.

Teenage boys were abducted and brought to the base. By the 1980s thousands of abducted boys had been used in the programme. Here they underwent terrible periods of physical and mental torture, in order to break their minds. Their minds were then reprogrammed. It is believed that many children were killed during the process, and their bodies buried on the site. Some of these children were released with mind programming, to be sleeper cells, and used to perform special missions at a later date. Abducted people were subjected to large amounts of electromagnetic radiation, to test mind control technology. A special chair was designed, known as the 'Montauk Chair', where someone could sit in it and have his mental and precipitory powers boosted. Psychics were also used for this project. Duncan Cameron was found to have psychic abilities, and was involved in many of the Montauk Chair experiments. While in the Montauk Chair he could manifest objects just by thinking about them. Preston Nichols was involved with the experiments on Duncan.

Al Bielek was a member of the team, and alleged that a boys programme not only travelled through time, but were the first to travel to Mars. The researchers at Montauk discovered that not only could they travel through time tunnels to Earth's past and future, but they could also travel to other planets, especially Mars. By utilizing the time tunnels, researchers could teleport to Mars. Duncan Cameron was able to teleport to one of the Mars pyramids, and open a portal inside, for one of these team of researchers. Al Bielek described the Martian bases as approximately 20,000 years old, that were constructed by human like extraterrestrials, that had left thousands of years ago.

Eventually Duncan used the Montauk Chair to manifest a creature from his subconscious mind. The 'Beast' materialized as a large hairy monster, roaming the base and destroying everything it could find. To get rid of the beast, the researchers had to smash equipment, cut cables and essentially wreck many years of research. They attempted to shut off the power to the base's transmitters which powered the chair. When the power source was cut, the beast dissipated from this plane of existence.

This occurred on August 12th 1983, and resulted in the Montauk Project being shut down. Everyone working on the project were deprogrammed, their minds were wiped clean. About a year after the event, a special operations unit purged the base, and removed anything they found to be too sensitive to abandon.

The Air Force took over the base in 1993, until 1997. The following year the Navy took over, it is believed that they were involved in particle beam weapon research. This would have been a continuation of the SDI, Star Wars' programme, originally set up by President Reagan in the 1980s. Jack Pruitt controlled the Montauk Project. He had previously been involved in Project Pegasus, which was a CIA/ DARPA teleportation and time travel programme, which ran from 1968-1972 .

NEW WORLD ORDER AGENDA

Phil Schneider believed that the 'New World Order', and the alien agenda, are one and the same. Some people refer to this as the 'One World Order'. He asserted that the alien agenda would be the complete takeover of the planet by, by killing off of 7/8 of the world population by 2029. Phil Schneider had attended two classified UN meetings at a deep underground military base outside New York. He discovered that Tall Grey extraterrestrials were dictating policies to the UN, and subsequently resigned his NATO position. The United Nations were obviously a front for this 'One World Order' agenda.

Phil Schneider's prediction over two decades ago may eventually become reality. With the coronavirus pandemic, much of the planet has been placed under lockdown. The draconian measures of governments worldwide, has resulted in restrictions of freedom of movement, extreme restrictions on freedom of speech, especially on Youtube and Facebook.

There are many theories as to the origin of this virus. China has a biological research laboratory in Wuhan, which was the first city to roll out the 5G network. This may well be a bioweapon attack by the Deep State/ Cabal to coincide with the deployment of 5G which can weaken the immune system.

Stewart Swerdlow, the last living survivor of the Montauk Project, said that this is a trick by the Deep State to incite fear and bring down the world's economy. With the worldwide lockdown, the Deep State's objectives are being realised. Their aims are:

1. Mandatory vaccination
2. Mandatory microchipping of the population
3. Abolition of cash-replaced by a digital currency
4. One World Government
5. Restriction of freedom of movement
6. Government arrogates the right to itself to decide which businesses may operate
7. Extreme restrictions on freedom of speech.

The cabal's plan is to control humanity, and 5G has enabled them to achieve their goal. The extremely high frequency waves, EHF, from satellites are irradiating the planet. The millimetre band up to 86 GHz is the most dangerous. At 60 GHz the body and blood cells cannot absorb oxygen, leading to serious lung infections and serious illnesses.

The 'One World Order' was planned many years ago. The final decision was taken in January 2020 in Davos, Switzerland, at the World Economic Forum. Agenda ID 2020 is an electronic ID program using vaccination as a platform for digital identity. In June 2019, China passed a law that rolled out a mandatory vaccination program. This came into effect on December 1, 2019. Mandatory vaccinations may also include DNA vaccinations and microchipping.

Nexus magazine, April 2020, stated that there is an hidden agenda to have everyone on the planet injected with a nanochip. This would then be linked to the 5G millimetre-wave network. These chips can be remotely charged with all your personal data, including bank accounts. In fact digital money is what they are planning. Dr Tedros, Director General of the World Health Organisation, recently said that the world must move towards digital money. Everyone would be tracked, every movement. The microchip program in Sweden is a cover for their mind control experiments. This is run by the Swedish military. Magnus Olsson, a businessman, received a nanochip implant in his brain unbeknown to him, when he went into hospital. He is now experiencing an acoustic attack, V2K daily. His remarkable story is on his website nanobrainimplant.com

Another important article on his website is: 5G will use the same frequency as military weapons do!

Denmark has also passed a new law for mandatory vaccinations. These new measures are the most extreme since the second world war.

It is obvious from the microchip program in Sweden, that it can be used for nefarious purposes by governments. Simon Parkes in the UK stated in one of his videos that vaccines might contain nano particles, which can be activated by microwaves similar to 5G transmissions.

The UN has also unveiled plans to implement Universal Biometric ID by 2030. Nearly every nation on Earth signed up for this plan, a universal agenda for humanity. This startling plan, a part of Globalisation, was virtually ignored by the international media. The New World Order envisaged by Phil Schneider is gradually being implemented.

EPILOGUE

During the last few years it is believed that many of the deep underground military bases have been destroyed. On Monday night, August 22nd 2011, a 5.3 magnitude earthquake struck a southern Colorado town called Trinidad. The region normally has hardly any seismic activity at all. The following day August 23rd, a 5.9 magnitude earthquake occurred 84 miles southwest of Washington D.C. This damaged the Washington Monument. Both these earthquakes were caused by sub-surface explosions, almost certainly nuclear devices. Whistleblowers have come forward to confirm this. Also seismographs of both these earthquakes clearly show a sudden jolt, indicative of an underground explosion, and not typical of normal earthquake activity. Each underground base held more than 30,000 people each, and there may have been up to 60,000 deaths.

The apparent nuclear strikes against underground military facilities were probably carried out by an international alliance, or Earth alliance. These are 'white hats' in the military who want full disclosure, and an end to the corruption and lies of the ruling elite. Many researchers including David Wilcock and Benjamin Fulford, confirm that there is a secret war to defeat the 'New World Order' agenda of the Deep State or Cabal. Some of these bases may have been controlled by Reptilians and Greys. The secret space programme whistleblower Corey Goode asserted that US troops were sent into Fema bases in early 2017, to take back control from Reptilians. Fema is an agency which is dedicated to responding to national emergencies. Fema bases are also known as DUMBS. This agency is part of the 'New World Order' agenda, and is controlled by the cabal.

In recent years there have been many false flag attacks, orchestrated by the Deep State. The most notorious is 9/11, which was organised by the cabal. According to the alternative magazine Nexus, US Department of Energy documents from 2003 were released, which proved that 9/11 was a nuclear event. The US Geological Survey's dust sample at the site, also indicated that the destruction of the twin towers was a nuclear event. There is now overwhelming evidence to confirm this. Many elements were found, including Barium and Strontium, Thorium and Uranium, Lithium, Lanthanum, Yttrium, Chromium and Tritium. The presence of Chromium and the radioactive isotope Tritium indicates a nuclear detonation. The towers were specifically designed to withstand the impact and destructive force of airline crashes. An enormous amount of energy would be needed to destroy the towers, and this was achieved by mini nukes.

This incident led to the 'fake war on terror'. Many whistleblowers have confirmed this, including Robert Steele. He was a CIA agent and worked for the USMC military intelligence. He is an important whistleblower, exposing covert intelligence agencies, illegal banking activities, false flag attacks, and the fake war on terror. He also asserted that the Oklahoma City bombing was a false flag event, and many European terrorist attacks were also false flag events.

Phil Schneider had also confirmed that the Oklahoma City bombing was a false flag attack. He said that the authorities stated that it was a nitrate or fertilizer bomb that caused the explosion. First they disclosed that it was a 1,000 pound fertilizer bomb. Then it was 1,500, then 2,000 pounds. Finally they said 20,000. Phil Schneider said that it's not possible to put 20,000 pounds of fertilizer in a Rider Truck. Schneider knew the chemical structure, and the application of construction explosives. He stated that a nitrate explosion would just have shattered a few windows in the federal building in Oklahoma City. Schneider categorically stated that the government had lied about the attack, and that it was a nuclear incident.

Phil Schneider was hired to do a report on the World Trade Centre bombing. The reason he was hired is because he knew about 90 varieties of chemical explosives. He examined the pictures taken after the blast, where the concrete was puddled and melted. The steel and rebar was extruded up to 6 feet longer than its original length. The authorities lied 100%, when they claimed it was a nitrate explosive that done the damage. Phil claimed that there is only one weapon that can do this damage, a small nuclear weapon.

Phil Schneider married Cynthia Marie Drayer Simon in 1987. The couple had met in June 1986 at a meeting of the Oregon Agate and Mineral Society. Phil and Cynthia later had a daughter, Marie Schneider. The marriage was a difficult one, and they divorced in 1990. There had been several problems in their relationship, the pressures of a new family, failed business, and physical problems. As Cynthia said,' we had a bad marriage, but developed it into a great friendship'.

Phil Schneider disseminated the truth, and paid the ultimate price in January 1996. Phil's legacy of truth and honesty still survives, more than two decades after his death.